I AM THANKFUL

An Adult Coloring Book for Mothers

By Elizabeth Ann Garvey

I AM thankful for my husband who is my friend and partner for life.

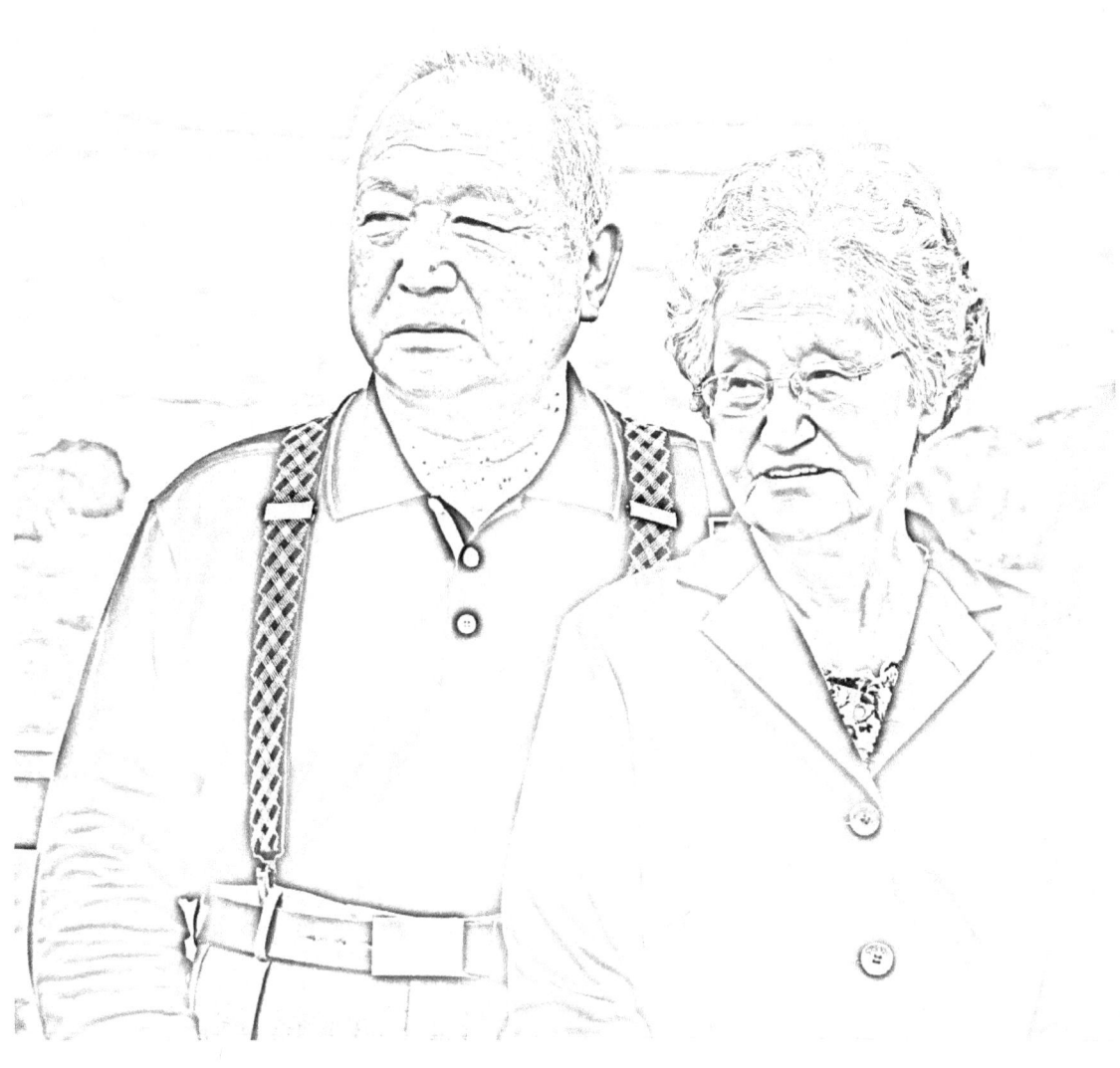

I AM thankful to hear a small voice in the night.

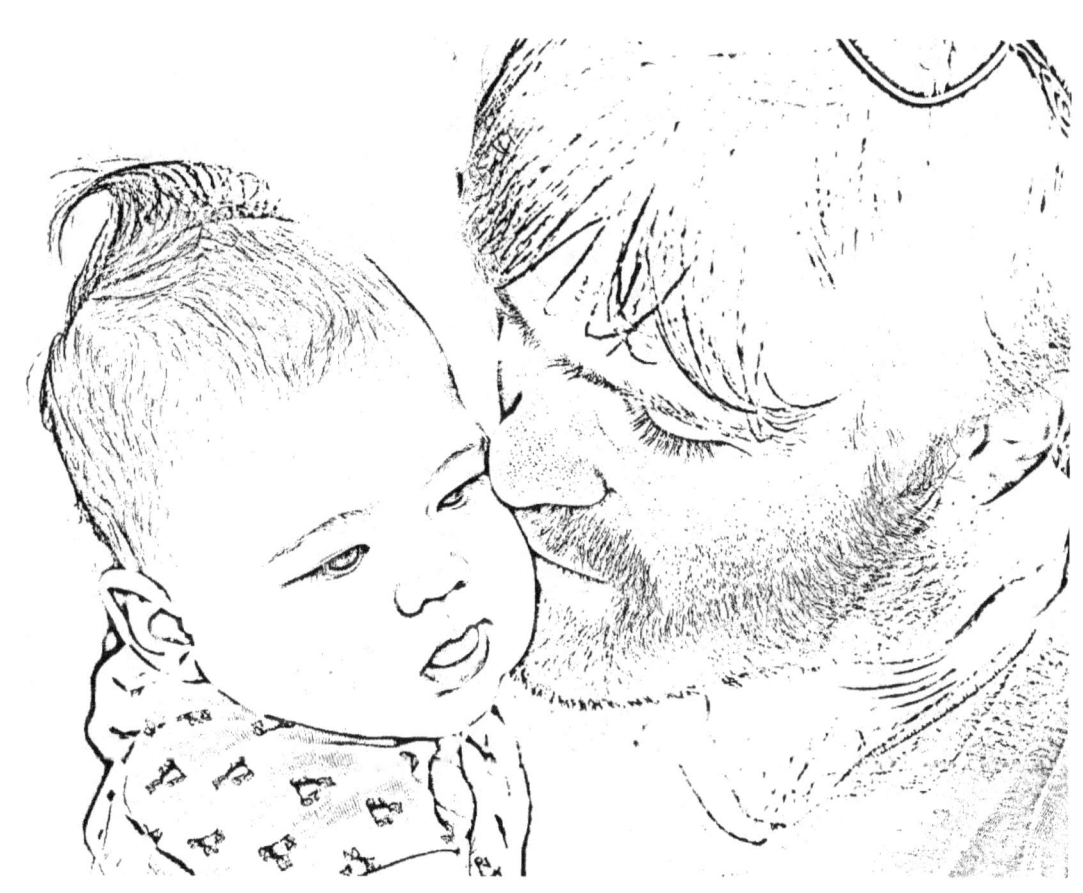

I AM thankful for games of peek-a-boo.

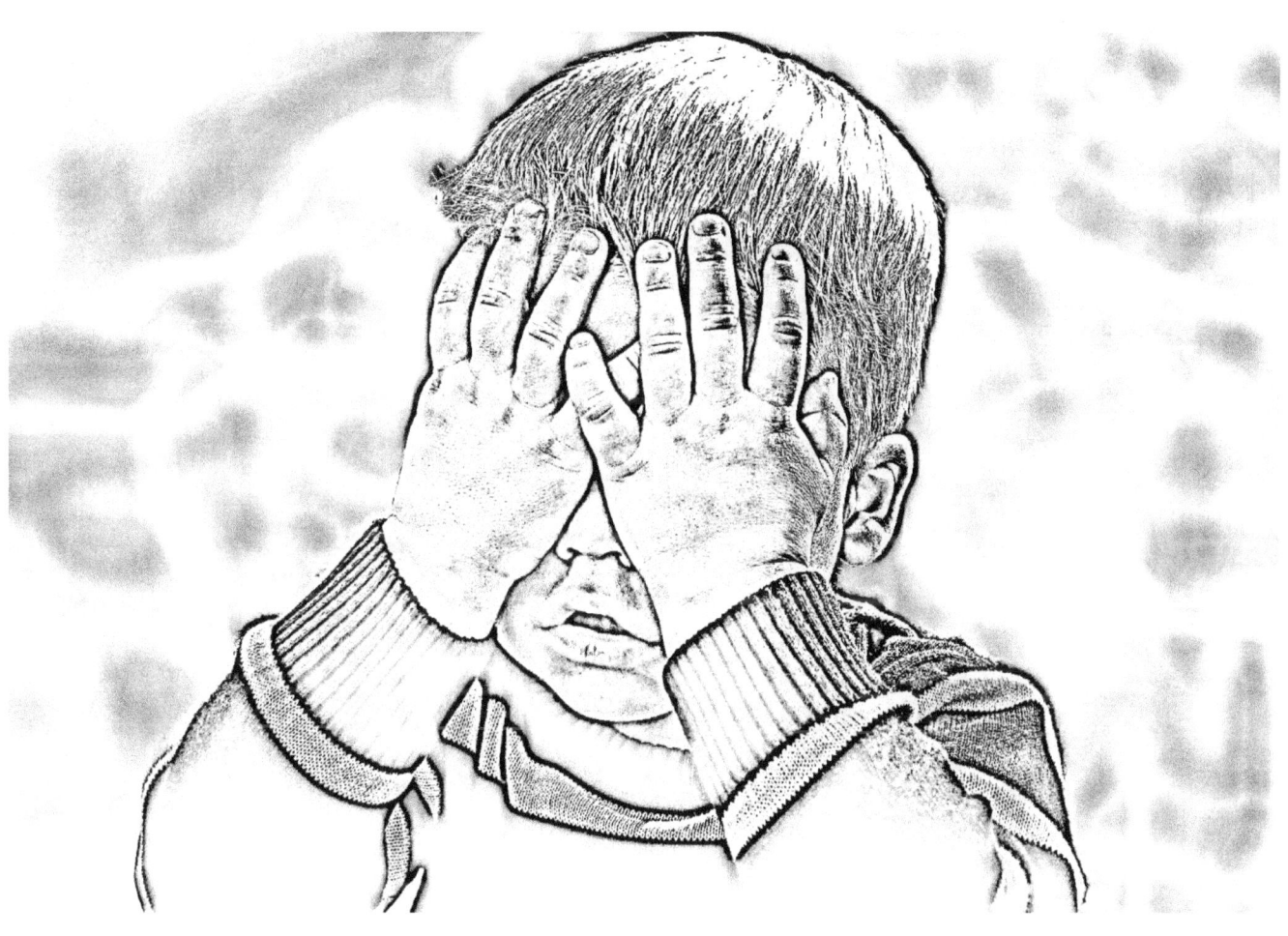

I AM thankful to help you.

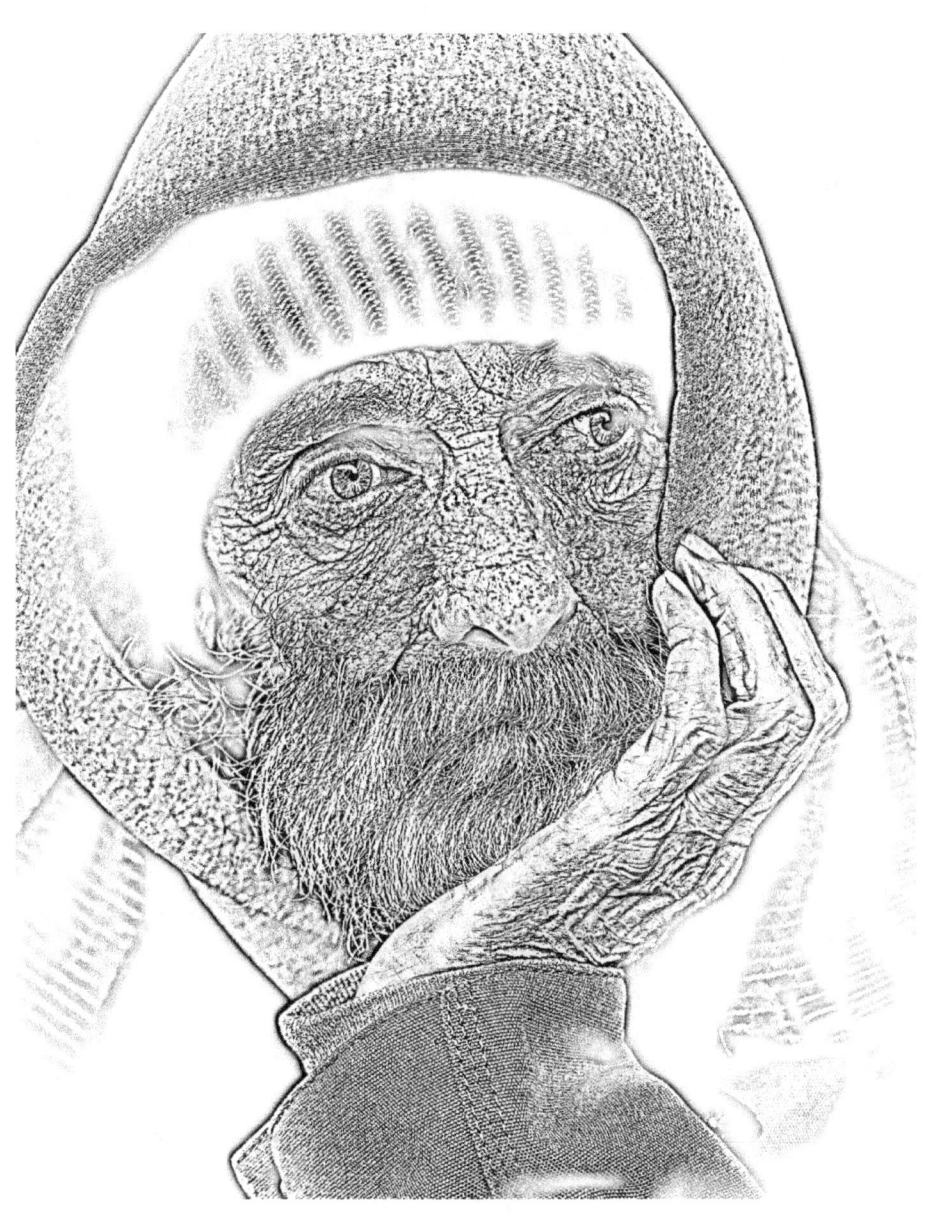

I AM thankful for this door for it means I have a home for my family.

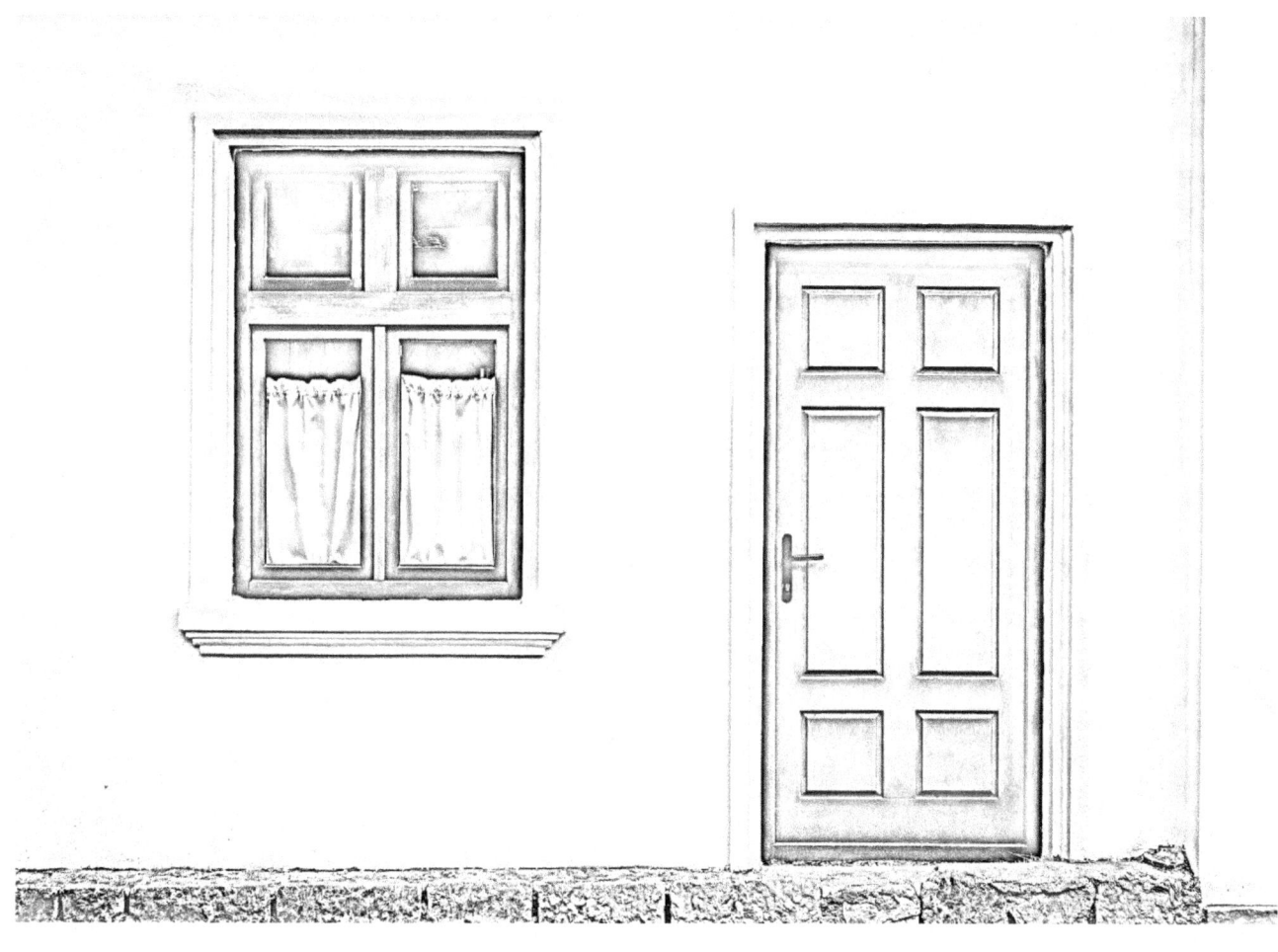

I AM thankful for a kitchen to clean and dishes to do because it means I was able to feed you.

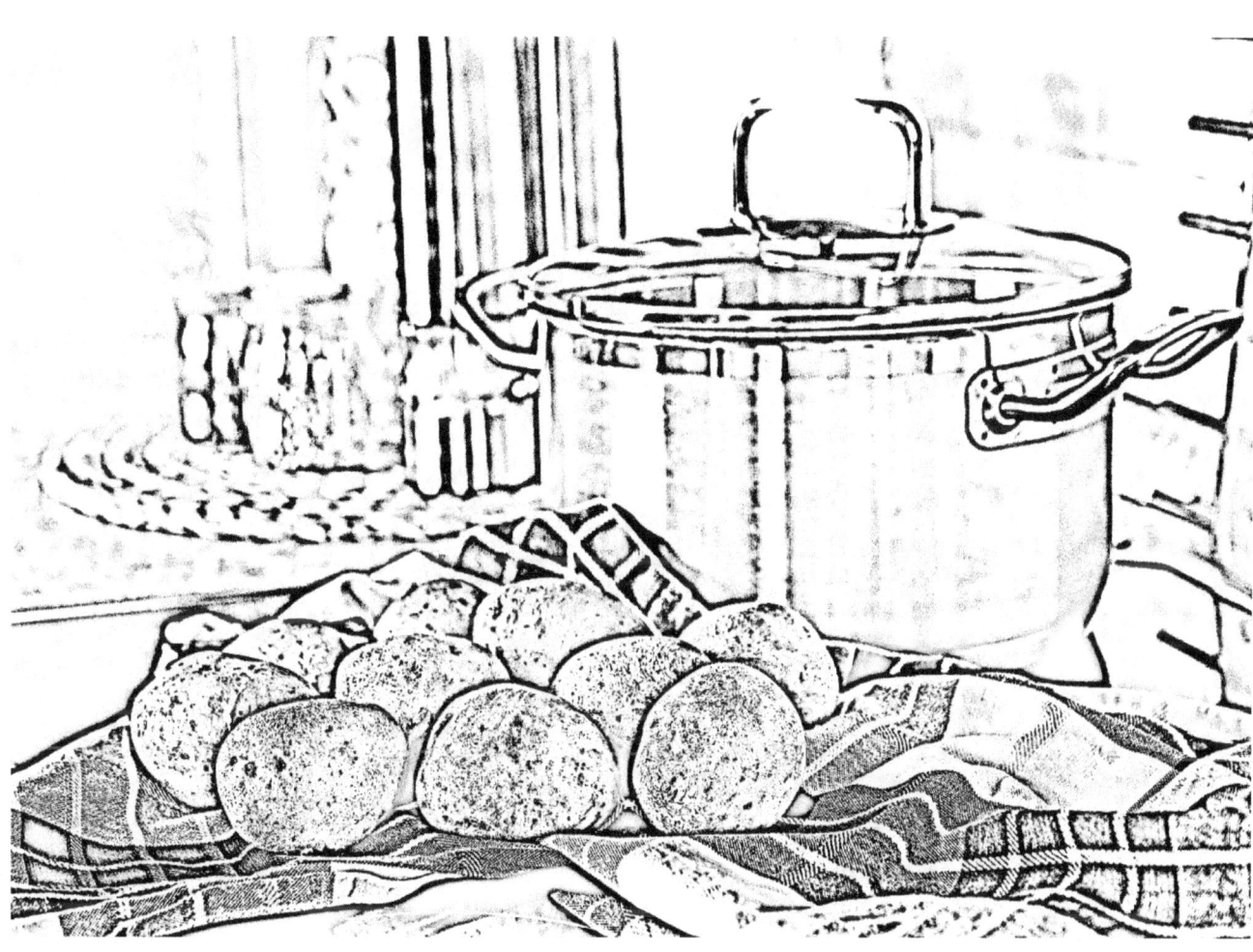

I AM thankful for a cup of tea and a little time for me.

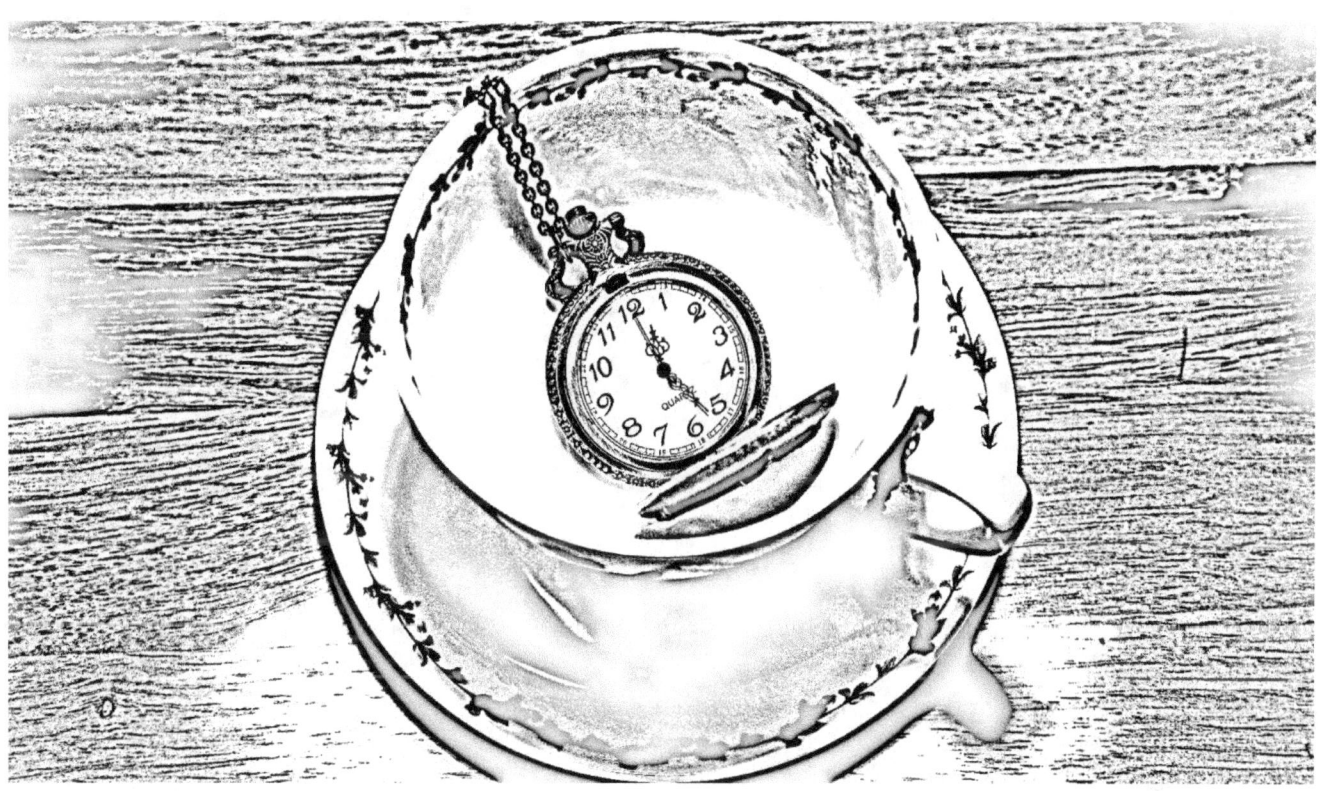

I AM thankful for this stack of journals because I have thoughts of value to share.

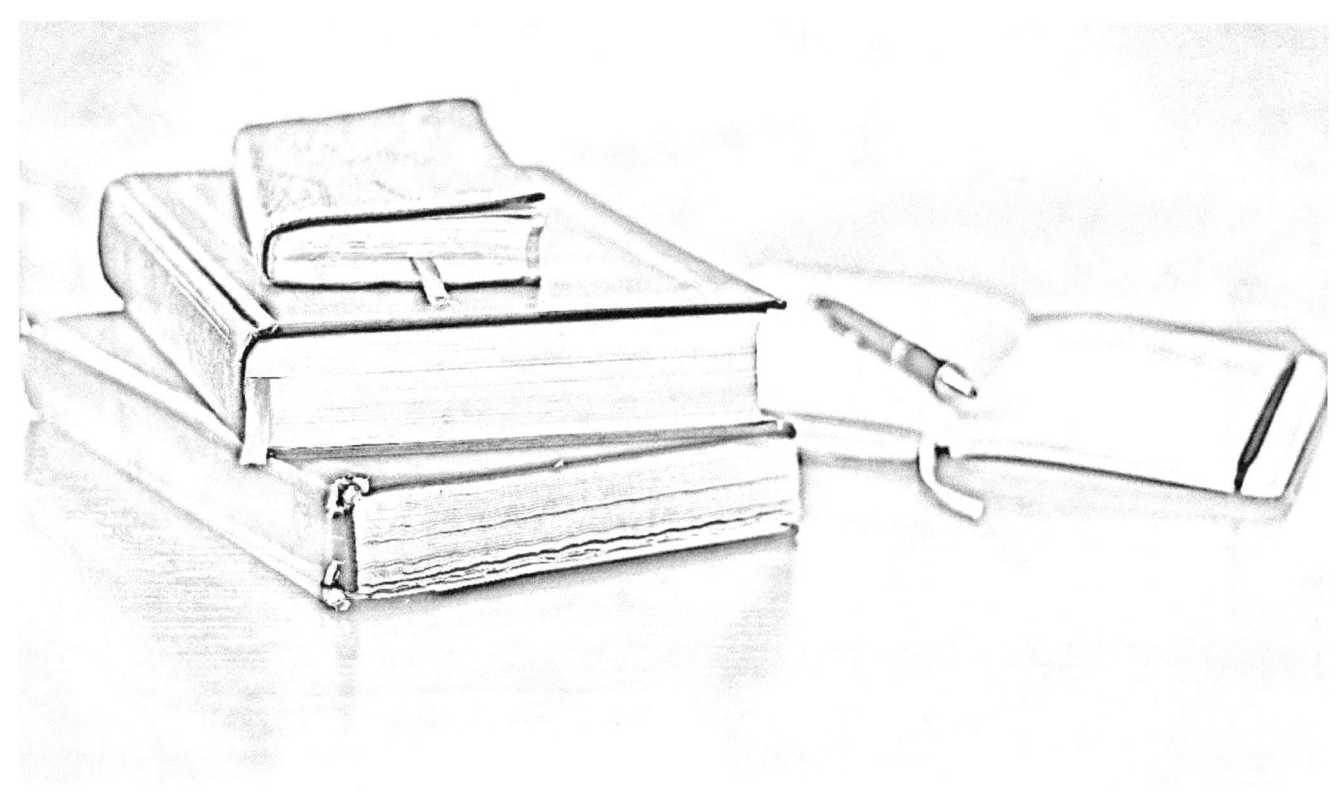

I AM thankful for apples and pears.

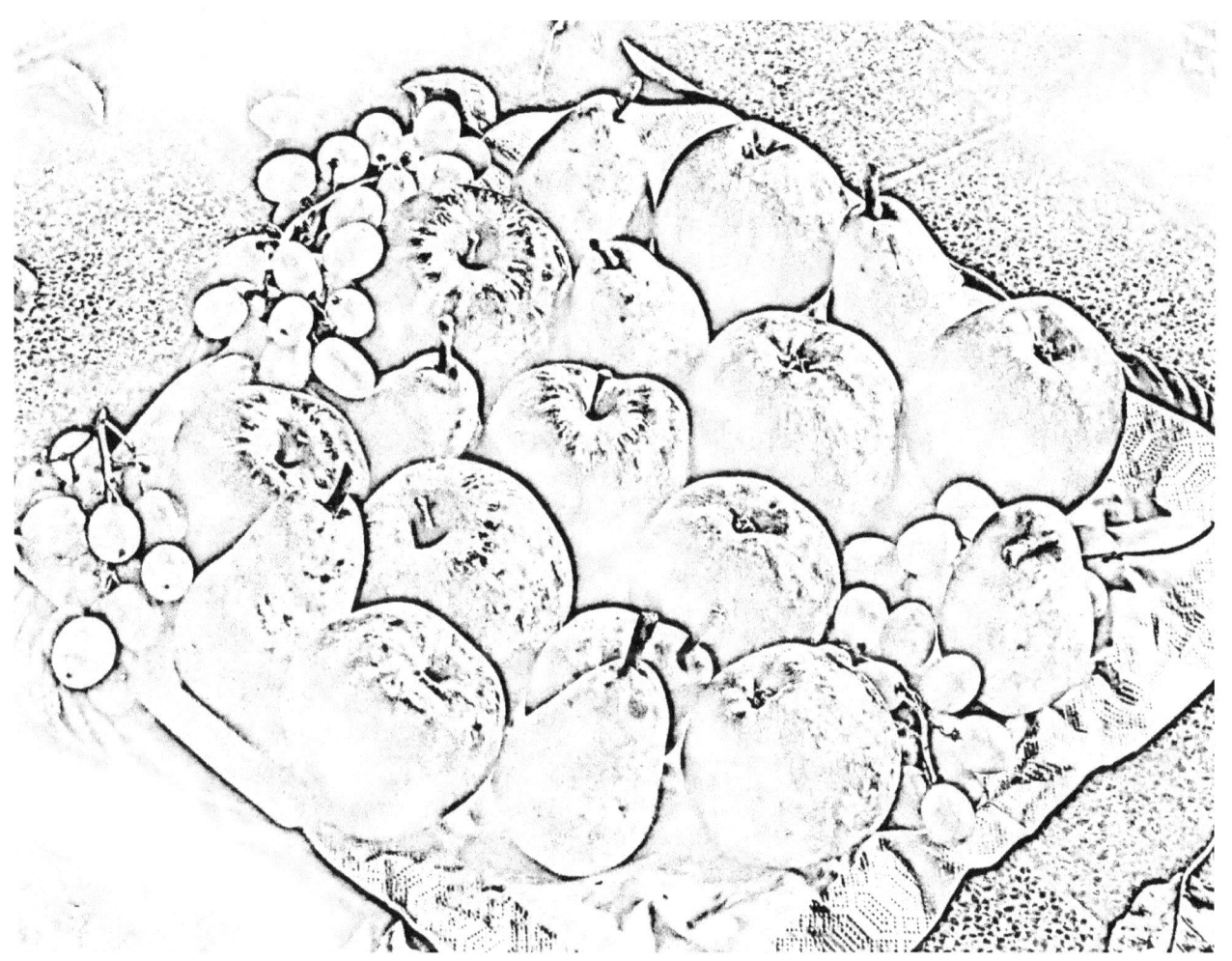

I AM thankful to know who I Am.

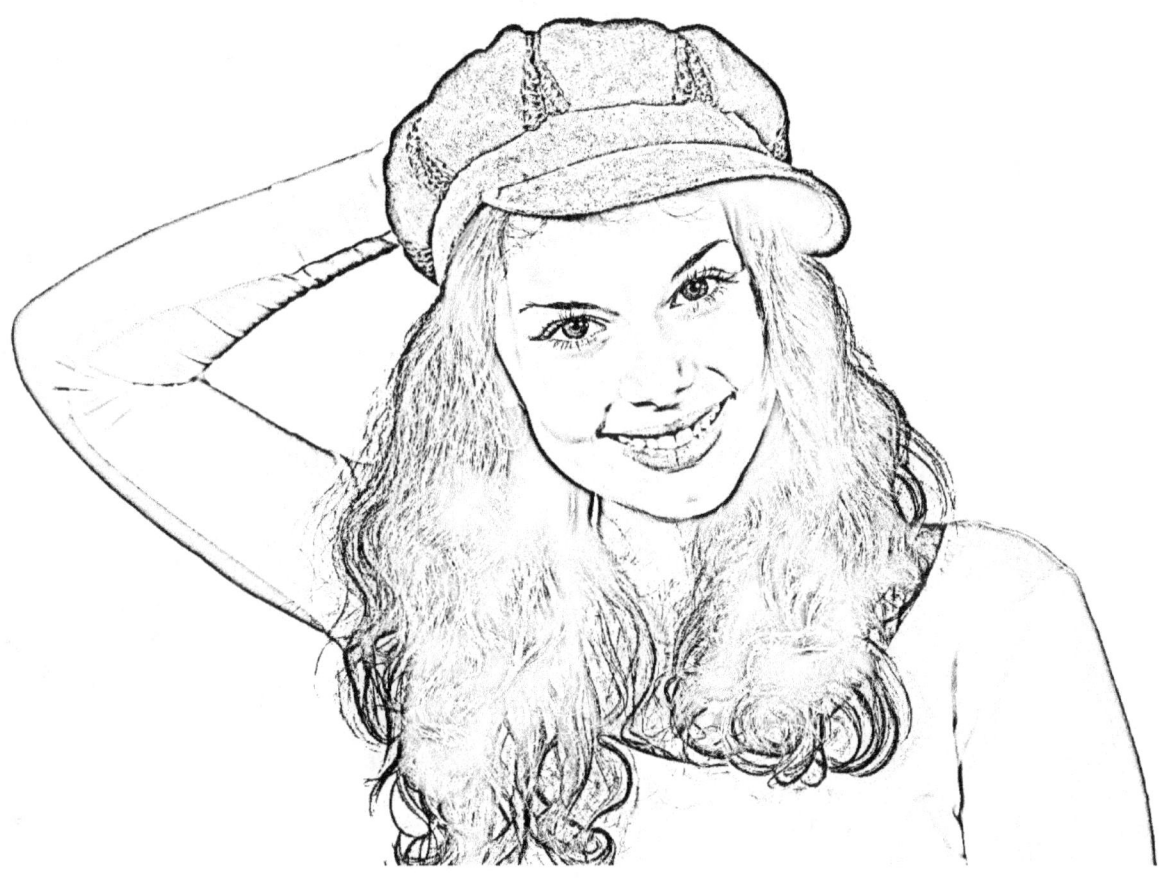

I AM thankful to be covered by the Lamb.

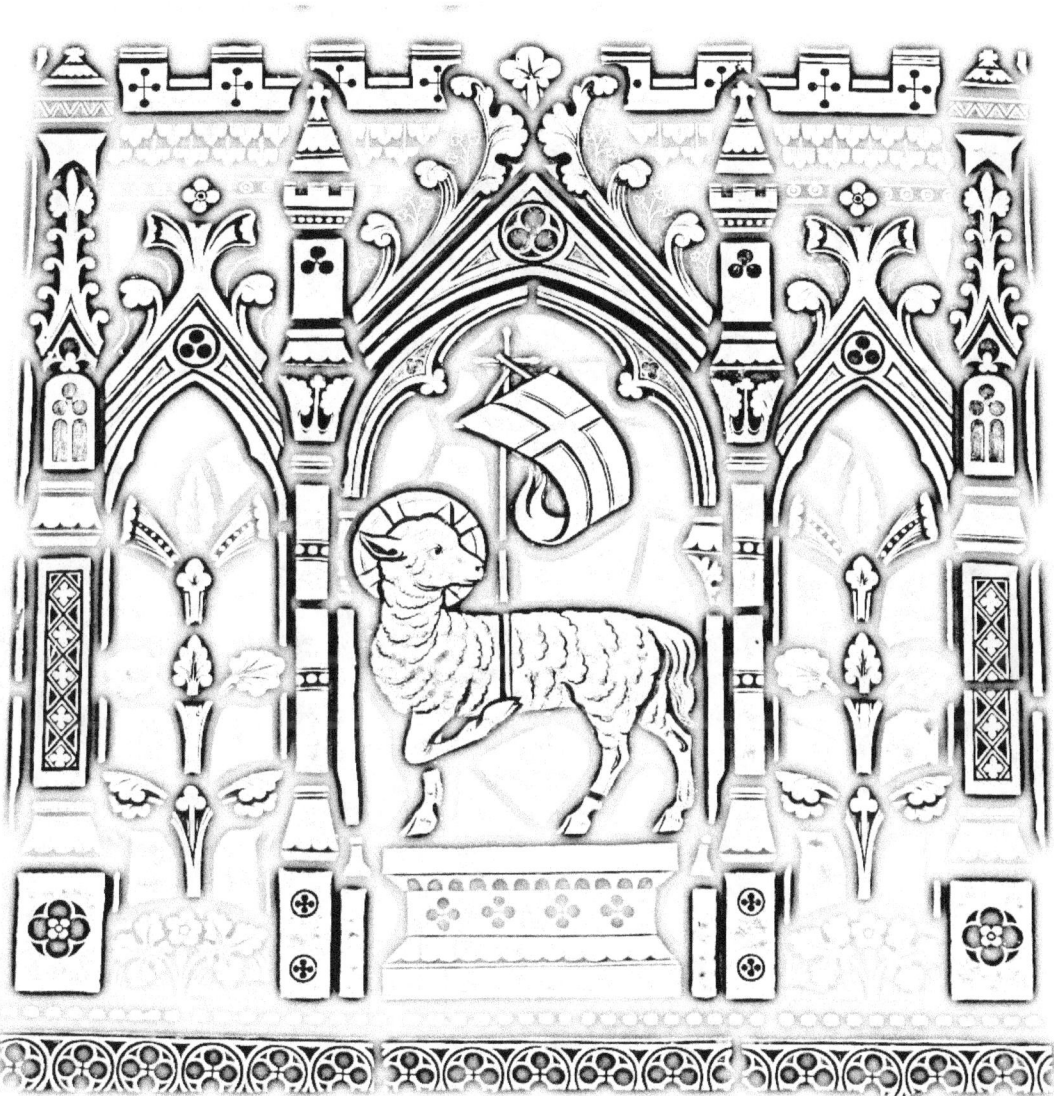

www.ingramcontent.com/pod-product-compliance
Lightning Source LLC
Chambersburg PA
CBHW081421170526
45166CB00010B/3431